Wolf Intervals

The Poiema Poetry Series

Poems are windows into worlds; windows into beauty, goodness, and truth; windows into understandings that won't twist themselves into tidy dogmatic statements; windows into experiences. We can do more than merely peer into such windows; with a little effort we can fling open the casements, and leap over the sills into the heart of these worlds. We are also led into familiar places of hurt, confusion, and disappointment, but we arrive in the poet's company. Poetry is a partnership between poet and reader, seeking together to gain something of value—to get at something important.

Ephesians 2:10 says, "We are God's workmanship . . ." *poiema* in Greek—the thing that has been made, the masterpiece, the poem. The Poiema Poetry Series presents the work of gifted poets who take Christian faith seriously, and demonstrate in whose image we have been made through their creativity and craftsmanship.

These poets are recent participants in the ancient tradition of David, Asaph, Isaiah, and John the Revelator. The thread can be followed through the centuries—through the diverse poetic visions of Dante, Bernard of Clairvaux, Donne, Herbert, Milton, Hopkins, Eliot, R. S. Thomas, and Denise Levertov—down to the poet whose work is in your hand. With the selection of this volume you are entering this enduring tradition, and as a reader contributing to it.

—D.S. Martin
Series Editor

Wolf Intervals

Graham Hillard

CASCADE *Books* · Eugene, Oregon

WOLF INTERVALS

The Poiema Poetry Series

Cascade Books
An Imprint of Wipf and Stock Publishers
199 W. 8th Ave., Suite 3
Eugene, OR 97401

www.wipfandstock.com

PAPERBACK ISBN: 978-1-6667-3174-3
HARDCOVER ISBN: 978-1-6667-2460-8
EBOOK ISBN: 978-1-6667-2461-5

Cataloguing-in-Publication data:

Names: Hillard, Graham.

Title: Wolf intervals / Graham Hillard.

Description: Eugene, OR: Cascade Books, 2022 | Series: The Poiema Poetry Series.

Identifiers: ISBN 978-1-6667-3174-3 (paperback) | ISBN 978-1-6667-2460-8 (hardcover) | ISBN 978-1-6667-2461-5 (ebook)

Subjects: LCSH: Poetry. | American poetry—21st century.

Classification: PS617 H55 2022 (paperback) | PS617 (ebook)

10/07/22

for Mary

Whither thou goest

Contents

III.

The *wolf* made itself heard in the days of unequal temperament.

Frederick Niecks
A Concise Dictionary of Musical Terms

The Forest

It's often in the woods that we can learn
The price of things, because it's often there
We see it paid. How many brambles caught
My skin that day, when I walked the familiar
Path other children had cut through the forest,
Fracturing saplings' slender bones and beating
The earth into a dull, compacted clay?
Did I know what I was careening toward
Each time a root leapt up and caught my shoe?
I must have been a tender seven or eight,
Newly allowed to roam the unfenced land
My father owned and the adjacent woods
Much loved by older boys. I didn't know
Their names, but I observed them from a distance
When I could, saw them train air rifles on
Squirrels, rabbits, each other, whatever moved
Or cast a shadow in that stippled light.
Perhaps they saw me, too. I couldn't say
What they desired or what they were prepared
To do to get it. I kept to myself
And left them to the mystery of age.
Until that morning, I was innocent,
Would not have hesitated to pursue
A trail of breadcrumbs to a witch's house
Or strike a bargain with a laughing imp.
I never thought to hide myself from harm.
If you look, you can see me through the trees,
Still stumbling toward the moment that would harden
Something soft in me, some unconsciousness
Of what all children must become in time.
The hare is only steps ahead of me
By now, its body like a piece of rope

1

That someone has sliced lengthwise with a blade.
Four sharpened sticks pin down its curling edges,
Exposing the ruined organs like a curse
That has already been pronounced, or like
An exhortation spoken with the strength
Of a thousand voices. I hear footsteps
Behind me, turn around. No one is there.
I look again, not old enough to know
That whoever did this has surely fled,
Will satisfy himself with guessing what
I must have believed in those awful seconds
Of discovery. I kick fallen leaves
Across the ravaged body, and I go.
Or, coward that I am, I simply run.
This poem is not theodicy, and God
Can do whatever he decides is just.
But I became a different child in those woods,
Slipped off a former life and stepped away
As if from a thin, ghostly suit of clothes.
I was not touched by anyone that morning.
Whatever hand I felt, I feel it still.

I.

Well Temperament

The pack steals into Köthen
   in darkness, drawn by

tones as pure as the teeth
   of children. Still,

the major second seems
   to howl, like the wolf

intervals of old, until
   pulled into consonance.

At night, exhausted,
   Bach steps away

from his score, leaving
   unmelted a leading note

that will not be
   resolved. In the silence

of that midnight, the alpha
   strides across the clavier

as if she means to play it.
   This is what is meant

by *Allegro*—see how swiftly
   she strikes the keys!

Bach dreams of such
   music and awakens

to unknown modulations.
  If he sees how

he must tame them, let him
  do it. We will

set the room to order
  as he works, seal

windows, sweep clumps
  of fur into the fire.

David and Bathsheba Share a Cigarette

He cups his hands around the flame of her.
He is the ember crushed into her palm.
She is the streak of tar along his teeth.
He is the palace corner where she stands.
She seals him with the moisture of her tongue
And grips him in her fingers soft and white.
He is the cells dividing in her lungs.
She is the vapor darkening his sight.
He warms the hidden places in her throat,
Makes love inside a chemical caress.
She is the nub end sealed with drying spit.
He is the slag and soot stain on her dress.
She is the catch and tremble in his breath.
She tastes of ash the way he tastes of death.

Mikhail Gorbachev Addresses an Auditorium of Southern Baptists

Jackson, Tennessee, 2000

Not a word will be remembered.
Only the expression on the great man's face
as he realizes that history has stranded him

in this détente with God-botherers. Gone
are the fluttering ambiguities of Reykjavik
and Geneva—in their place the orthodoxies

of bankers, surgeons, Americans
whose money has swept him across
an ocean. Fourteen years ago, Chernobyl

shuddered and unclasped its hands,
released its beakless bird. Now, even
the interpreter seems singed, consumed

by the fission of the past as he unties
each Slavic knot, pronouncing
the unpronounceable as the audience chews.

Gorbachev's speech proclaims peace.
In his mind, he restrings barbed wire,
murders Wałęsa, fires into Hungarian crowds

as they flee to the West. Over coffee
as weak as Soviet petrol, those gathered
rejoice in their eternal triumph,

a dispensation that can never be
altered. None knows what is coming,
and none will be convinced

of any truth beyond what he has paid
to hear, unassailable assurance
that we, even we, are blessed.

Theodicy

A male black bear has been released back into the wild after state wildlife agents tranquillized it and removed a plastic jar that was stuck on its head. —The Associated Press

Tongue leathered and stiff with thirst,
   starving, he stole nightly onto

main streets, town squares, pawed
   storefront glass rich with moonlight,

watched mannequins in evening gowns
   stare darkly ahead, blind as earth. Filthy,

sick with the stench of his breath, he
   swung at air, birdsong, nothing,

pried the dull lip an inch from his neck—
   hard purchase—and relented. When

nothing else remained to be done, he lay
   in the crusting mud of the creek bank

and lapped, ounce by ounce, the water
   that seeped into the jar. The end,

when it came, was quiet: dart's prick
   and darkness, rain cold as stone, gust

of wind—a mercy—and forgetting. How
   quickly he returned to his forest then, freed

for a time from the impulse to question,
   as all those are who have been spared.

Benediction

Because I will not raise my hands to take
The benediction from the pastor's lips,
My daughter stands beside me, lifts my arms—
Two dead men whom she means to resurrect.
She cannot fathom my contrariness,
Uneasy virtue camouflaged as vice,
Nor license what must seem like unbelief,
Refusal to accept a gentle law.
The truth is something knottier than that:
Spontaneous conviction polished hard.
The pulpit offers rest while I seek work.
My labor is the labor she performs,
My blessing her capacity for grace,
My good word the petition on her face.

Honeysuckle

I could never
have enough
of spring candied
and sealed
with a bulb,
sweetened dew
a stamen's length
from my fingers—
crystal tip

of a magician's
wand, softer than
a gloss of foam.
Understand,
to keep it
from my lips
was to delay
one of the
few pleasures

granted
a lonely child,
who sat
in hell's mown
grass, broiling,
wanting
a honeysuckle
drop to cool
his tongue.

Genealogy

Clara

You bloomed in insect season, skin-sealed, limbs
slight as the wings of the cicadas that plagued us

through early summer, droned endless Our Fathers
outside steamy windows and surrendered themselves

to the flat, cracked expanse of the driveway. Night phlox,
you opened in darkness: amniotic sky moonless

and still as the unstirred air of the house where we waited,
flesh gathering dew, joy throbbing in our guts,

for you. Mute crescendo, you swelled and summoned yourself
into being—bundle of rag and cord, hard lump.

When you arrived, the doctors told us that, because your eggs
were already in place, not only our daughter but our grandchildren

had been born, as numerous as the bodies I'll sweep
from the sidewalk in the last moments before sunset.

Proverb

with lines from an English nursery rhyme

When the wind is in the north,
the skilful fisher goes not forth.

When the wind calls from the firth,
the larkspur melts into the earth.

When the wind is damp with rain,
the yearling stalks the sugarcane.

When the wind is at a gale,
the muck seeps from the poison shale.

When the wind cuts through the fog,
the witches boil the newt and frog.

When the frog stews in the pot,
the Shorthorn's cream begins to clot.

When the heifer bears a calf,
the master strikes it with a staff.

When the master falls to sleep,
his sons and daughters flee his keep.

When the rain besieges them,
the parson's wife intones a hymn.

When the rain is yellow foam,
the woodchuck burrows through the loam.

When the loam is only sand,
the wolf sings in the barren land.

When the wind is in the east,
  'tis neither good for man nor beast.

Ezekiel on the Somme

Ezekiel 37:1–10

In sunset hours the prophet feeds his army,
Assigns them rank, digs trenches, and draws up
A battle plan. Of course this infantry
Of bones and flesh and breath will need their gas masks,
But what of ammunition, proper boots,
A letter from a sweetheart passed along
From man to man to cheer the lot? The guns
Have swallowed whole brigades already. Soon,
The day will break on fields no god has blessed,
That yield no lesson for an oracle
Or teacher. Will it be a crime to send them
Across that stretch of dismal ground to be
Fragmented? No worries. The Lord has made them.
It will be he who tears their bones apart.

Christ Walks on the Adventure River Wave Pool

Memphis, 1989

How strange to see myself submerged that day,
As if enacting an afflictive dream
Of drowning. Memory can place me there,
On the blue-concrete apron of the pool,
But how I drifted past all reach or reason
Is mystery, the stuff of midnight sweat
And prayer: *Yea, though I swam*, et cetera.
I know I thought that I was going to die,
Saw sunlight on the surface like a rope
That snapped with each new wave, each pummeling
That swept me, nine years old, below again.
What happened? Who but God can say? And yet
I know I heard his footsteps on the water,
Felt hands that weren't my own bearing me up.

The Marine

I shouldn't be watching him,
  the young man who steps

from his father's truck into
  the clamor of the airport's

drop-off lane—the traffic
  pushing past a rush

of headlights, a blur of noise.
  Already his posture has begun

to harden, the tightness
  in his shoulders to signal

the resignation of his body
  to wills beside his own,

other hands. This
  is the last ritual of a life

to be set aside:
  his father's grim, proud

nod; a final blessing
  as reverent as the three generations

of crosses that mark
  their genealogy in some

country church, its land
  leased in perpetuity.

Beside his feet, his luggage
    sits as perfectly aligned

as the sight on his M4,
    his recession from the world

creeping now into his gestures
    as he tells his mother

some fraction of what
    she requires. Even to make

a narrative of this moment
    is to confound it,

to drape with the smothering
    cloth of the symbol

the rifle's clean lines
    and oiled mouth.

To their left a car honks
    to speed them along,

its driver waving his arms
    before comprehending

and shaking his head,
    eyes wide with the horror

of recognition, as if
    in his thoughtlessness

he has bound himself
    to some darker impulse,

his alone rather than ours,
    all of ours, mine.

Wolves

It had long been Stalin's habit, while hosting important visitors,
to doodle wolves' heads on a pad in red pencil. —The Cold War: A
New History

He begins, always, with the eyes—a poet's trick
   of distillation. Only when he has made them

perfect does he grade the cheeks,
   cast muzzle and brow. Finished, the face

is ravenous, fresh from the throat
   of its prey. He admires the terror in its jaw

and feeds it into the fire. Today, I tip a book
   of wolves from the highest shelf of a secondhand

store, brush the dust from its mangled pelt,
   and find them staring: Eurasian Gray,

Egyptian Jackal—all drawn with what could be
   a child's incautious hand. Even in effigy

they startle, seem to tremble with a murderous
   intention. In Scandinavian legend,

the skin of the female is pared into a girdle.
   The wearer, driven before a need to devour,

howls. A stranger to this knowledge,
   Stalin can only pause as Russia sleeps

behind him, a yearling in the lap of Europe—
   can only crumple her edges, begin again.

Class Outing, Kunstmuseum Basel, Switzerland

They had thought themselves immune, these minor sinners
on a half-day lark. Even the Old Masters had aroused
the tight inwardness of boredom, private as any grief
lest *der Lehrer* see. Whichever of them spied first
the broken man upon his shroud said nothing,
nudged the ribs of a smaller boy, conceived a joke
he dared not say, cautiously sneered. Only
in their tutor's purposed step did they discern
that some malevolence had crept among them, a tempting spirit
to be cast off with sternness too conspicuous to miss.
Now they leaned toward it. Here was faith reduced
to meat: Holbein's *Body of the Dead Christ in the Tomb*
placed brazenly before them as if to answer
childish certainties. Worst of all was Christ's commonness:
his form, entirely blessed, reduced to this
wan slab; his eyes a ghoul's, unsighted, cast heavenward
in vain; his feet filthy. Of this, no priest could know
a thing. The artist had tramped to hell for a glimpse
of the vision. Eventually, the spell broke, as such
things must. Other rooms awaited. The swiftness
of their departure then was a kind of prayer.

Slaughterhouse Pond

Sleepless, the fish wait
  for the steer's head:
    the apprentice's arcing

heave, the silvery shattering
  of the surface as, at last,
    their prize appears. By the time

it descends to them, its mute
  bewilderment has relaxed
    into nothingness, and even that

is soon lost to the fever
  of their feeding. The skull,
    stripped clean, glides down

to the pond bed, awaits
  its dredging, rescuing, bleaching,
    sale. While it is with them, they will

brush against it but evade its gaze
  —its watchfulness like a god's
    as they circle and finally school . . . .

Pope Calixtus III Excommunicates Halley's Comet: Rome, 1456

Pressed by neighbors, family, strangers, those present
would recall first his voice, thin as the beer doled out
by the orphans of crusading fathers. Only the canniest
would note his body, holy and blessed, wasting in secret
beneath vestments stripped of the jewels needed
for swordsmiths' wages. The truth was something more
than that grim minutiae of the flesh, but how tell it:
that a dying man, sonless even by whores,
had gibbered to the wind, cast the heavens into hell?
That chronicler of popes, Bartolomeo Platina,
would later write that "the hairy and fiery star" had augured
calamity, but what dead child could be restored
by its absence? On the twelfth day, the comet disappeared
into rumor and memory, the certainty of witches. The women,
exhausted from their labors, went grumbling to the markets.

The Other Thief

Not the one who asked to be taken
with Christ into paradise, but the one
who smoldered on his cross, bid
himself abandon his body
before its last betrayal: usurpation
of a will he meant to keep
until the very end, expression as it was
of his terrible, damning dignity.

Elemental

Summer days, the neighbor boys would share our acres,
bring baseball gloves, tick spray, curse words intricate as gears

turning. Landless, they loved our fields, prized especially
the hours after rain, when all of us could scoop handfuls

of earth newly silkened, pull worms, still writhing,
from sodden clumps. I remember what it was not to understand

how something elemental—so obvious, so owed—
could give such pleasure, as any child might who had never

known its absence. How even then they must have sensed
a yielding, dirt creeping into their bones like marrow,

first portent of a distant, welcome shattering.

Roman à Clef

Desiring a symbol, the filmmaker leaves
   in his frame a pear that has begun to rot, sharp canker

upon the table at which the lovers sit, staring in turn
   at the sickly-sweet fruit from which an eruption must come:

froth and enzymes, the corruption of the body. At home,
   the filmmaker's child is dying. His wife has run a cord through

the flesh of the fruit of her orchard, unbodied heads shrunken
   and bobbing. She has hung it over their bed as a talisman.

II.

The High Branch

to a childhood friend

Of course I believed you when you claimed
   you could hang longer from the high branch

of the live oak that divided the field, marking
   that place as certainly as a fissure—the roots,

your father told us, as long as a dozen grown men.
   Still, we did what we had to do, toed again

footholds deepened by this habit, grasped limbs
   as known to us as our bodies, changeless

in an unremitting season. I knew even then
   it was fear that kept us, sealed our hands

to the perpetual bark so that we dangled, slim,
   uninverted bats, from that height. That the fall

was only the first of many partings, a pain
   so sharp I could almost teach myself to want it.

Paean (After George Peele)

His helmet now shall make a hive for bees.

His breastplate is an adder's rasping bed,
His boot a nest in which a songbird sleeps.
A red-tailed fox may summer in his greaves,
And geldings scrape their hooves against his skirt.

His rerebrace makes a home for sullen mice,
A curving roof against a summer rain.
An intricate poleyn may guard a dove,
Or gauntlets shield a rabbit's pulsing nest.

His flesh will feed a thousand pimpernels,
His skeleton a phlox's astral bloom.
An eel may dine upon his castoff heart,
His liver make a feast for famished boar.

His heaven is unwavering delight,
His soul an angel's weeping revelry.
Inside his chest is music fit for song,
His dignity the songbird's morning flight.

After Reading 'Reynard the Fox'

What to make of this villain
who ruins the wolf's wife, tears skin
from the face of a bear? Have we improved
since folklore wrung from our anxieties
such a creature, who will not confess
the Faith but catches by the throat
the faithful hare?
     This afternoon, in the lowest
patch of yard, beneath the windows
we keep sealed, the midges betray
one another to our poison. Their king
sends scouts who do not return
but leave their bodies on our flawless mat
of grass.
  Tonight
our offspring will thrash one another
about the heads, spill tears
like shimmering dew. What appalling love
we have for these children
who gather themselves, draw us sweetly
into their confidence, and lie.

31

Snow Day

"How the cold makes us dream!" —*Mary Oliver*

Coming in,
  the children
    are thin candles
  singed at one end,

their faces
  wicks
    the world has
  lit. What is

delight but this
  light in their
    skin?—a flame
  that will not

be snuffed:
  enough for
    a morning,
  a night—

a life.

Grammar School: Janitor

He must have dreamed of murdering us, hated the screaming,
    writhing mess we couldn't help but be, our pompous refusal

to meet his eye, or to be silent when he swept our sick,
    sawdust-dried, into the waiting pail. Even then, we didn't know

his name, though surely we had heard it used by teachers
    pregnant with some complaint or other: one more task

he would have to do before whistling away, his music
    tuneless, inscrutable, unmistakable, fierce.

At the National D–Day Memorial

Bedford, Virginia

Like a wound, or a medal pressed into a widow's hands,
it lies upon the landscape, one hundred acres

called to attention, gathered into such stillness
that even the birds seem wary of it, flitting away before

I can name them. The names one finds here
are artifacts, antique as ration coins: Vester, Eldridge,

boys innocent in the telling they have left us
along with this bronze necrology, careful arch

on which our dead are graven. Nearly everyone
who knew them is gone. Soon the names will be

mere letters, codes for which the cipher has been lost,
knowable only by this context: sculpture park,

gardened plaza where even now Eisenhower gazes
toward Normandy, his face as white as England's

chalk horses. I don't know if I can claim this
suffering, this desperate victory. Beneath the Overlord Arch,

the *Ad commemorandum* has begun to fade. Soldiers
sprint, frozen, through early tide. Above a stairway, men

of the 2nd Ranger Battalion scale Pointe du Hoc without
ceasing. Wherever I stand, they will not meet my eye.

The Timpanist

Ever watchful, the timpanist stoops,
   runs his palm over calfskin smooth

as undisturbed water, troubles
   its surface, judges the pitch. His hands

are fine-boned as something sculpted;
   they tremble as he keeps the count

he has taught himself to live by, has found
   in the pulse of the car's engine,

the metronomic dryer's click. In his grasp,
   the mallet waits, poised like lightning

gathering. Now he watches the flautist rise
   to solo, marks each phrase that glides,

winged, into the concert hall to nest
   among men in ties and jackets, ladies

roasting in furs. When it comes, his entrance is
   nearly nothing: a burst of gunfire,

a single, slim measure's roll to forte marking
   the final refrain. And he is startled,

the performance finished, to find himself
   among those called to their feet, singled out

by the conductor's raised hand as if patience itself
   could account for such music—as if love.

Morning Drop-Off

Desmond

Outside the Cumberland Presbyterian church,
   the air tasted of fresh tar, the sweat of the men

who seemed to lay it daily. I watched their black lake crest
   then turned my eye to the dog treeing squirrels

in neighboring grass, his teeth like a seam
   where someone had knitted him together.

In the back seat, my son pressed against his window,
   its glass a bubble that could not be made to pop,

shouting *run, run!* but meaning *kill, kill!*, his chant
   a pure stream into which some blood had spilled.

Cleanse it? No, I lapped it up! What pleasure
   to dip my head in it, drink deeply, thirst no more.

Proverb

A borrowed apple will not rot,
    nor hangmen's ropes concede a knot,

nor burning leaves remit their flames,
    nor truant boys give up their names.

The wobbly stool will not bear weight,
    and neither must the broken gate.

A fence will overrule no thief.
    A priest may die in unbelief.

An idle wolf will kill a child,
    but only if the winter's mild.

A yellow cardinal augurs snow,
    the shallow wave an undertow.

A calf that splits its hoof must die.
    (Be sure the villagers comply!)

An ill-formed babe must not be touched,
    nor any palsied hand be clutched.

Old men may live on salted fish
    if served from an embroidered dish.

The wisdom of a witch is sure,
    but you must pay for any cure.

A lisping tongue shall be pulled out.
    Do not permit complaint or doubt.

A fool may well advise a king,
but do not tell him anything.

After Flooding

I could see it through a dozen seasons of mending,
the water line so high it might have been fashioned
by sparrows: hieroglyphics beaked
onto rose gum bark, awaiting translation.

I knew, of course, the truth as others
knew it: that flooding stirred the river's bottom,
dredged mud as white as bone dust and left it,
roadmap of catastrophe, on branches, trunks,

leaves corrupt as corpses. How could I refuse
to follow it, pursue its paths luckless and fraught?
How neglect this distillation—primitive as weather,
patient as the slow receding of water?

Balletomane

In sharp contrast to the public spectacle surrounding the former tsars' appearances at the ballet, audiences and dancers never quite knew when Stalin might appear or which of his surrogates might be there, watching. —Apollo's Angels: A History of Ballet

First the murmuring, then the air
turned peculiar: the sudden, stifling
closeness of two thousand breaths
drawn and held
like the fermata before an entrance.
Though no one can be certain
of his presence, all know
at such a time to fall
silent, to press themselves
against seatbacks
polished by decades of shoulders,
incline their heads toward the stage
and await the safety of music,
the violins compelling the movement
of the dancers. To survive
is to be still: to see
without seeing the bulletproof box
nestled at stage right, its shelves
stocked with vodka and cigarettes,
each unknowable man within
a single, thoughtless error away
from a traitor's death. Above,
the three-tiered chandelier
sparkles, lends brilliance to pinewood
plucked from Siberian forests,
gold bought on the backs
of serfs long perished, insensible
to the cries of revolution,
the glorious dates—1871, 1905,

40

1917—woven into the curtain's
fabric. From this stage,
Lenin pronounced the birth
of a new country. Now,
dancers plié and tour. Men grip armrests,
order their affairs. Outside, Moscow
braces for winter as workers crush
against the Bolshoi's walls, desperate
to hear the footfalls
of the ballerinas, the closing notes
ephemeral as moonlight, the applause
so thunderous, so sustained,
it seems to go on for hours.

The Censor

When an Iranian Jew tells me that, in the nineties,
the man who censored films for the regime was blind—
that his assistant, a teenage boy, had to describe

to his master every frame that might make imperfect
their revolution—I think, *of course*. What better metaphor
could there be for such foolishness? How else

might God express what must be, what has to be,
his outrage? Only later do I think of the boy's terror,
if terror he had, about what slipped by him—what he,

in his innocence, must sometimes have failed to report.
With what relief, what unburdened joy, he must have sunk
to his prayers at the call of the muezzin. To what

sweeter sightedness he must have opened his eyes,
love for the holy like a brand upon his breast, a mark
he could be known by, and that would never heal.

The Polygrapher

Captain of an army of questions,
confederate of sweat, he will vanquish

all before him. Or timid, burrower
in a nest of tubes, he is mouselike,

deferential as the air within
the pneumograph. A liar,

I have seen him draw a spark
from skin, set a gland

afire. In his hand is clutched
a shock of nerves, small grains

he will gather to his table.
When his invitation comes, I dress

in scrolling paper, black needles
in my pockets, a tack turned upward

in my shoe. I test it with the tender
flesh of my foot, hear my pulse

protest. His study, arousal, is ancient,
secret as the promises of maidens.

Devotee of their language of shudders,
he will know them each in turn.

Manchineel

In the small hours, a dog
comes desperate to the noxious
fruit, a crop that cannot
be gathered. The blisters rise
in her throat. She curses
the place and leaves her bones
as warning.
       I have heard
the very smoke can blind
if the tree is burned, a drop
of sap raise boils. We mustn't
yield to its seducement, put
our tongues upon the bark
like this, or this, or this.

This

vale of tears.
This proving ground.
These choking fears.
This angel's sound.
This looping road.
Constricted fist.
This baffling code.
Peculiar bliss.
This effervescent
bubbling up.
This overflowing
measuring cup.
This poison world
and hateful sky.
This hidden pearl.
This joyful cry.
This promise that
will not be kept.
This welcome mat
on which I slept.
This balance none
can ever pay.
This loaded gun.
This disarray.
This preciousness
and desperate loss.
This evening dress
with silver cross.
This bead of sweat.
This makeshift bliss.
Eternal debt.
Enchantment. This.

Body Found in Churchill Downs Barn

headline

For hours, police tramped the already hardened dirt, too many
of them to be useful, pulled into labeled bags straw sodden
with blood, knelt and examined the corpse, rigor long upon it,
or stood murmuring in corners, workless, coffee clenched
in hands. Even after they have gone, the barn cannot be
made tidy. In their stalls, the horses buck, refuse the morning
grain, will not be led to pasture. What they have seen will soon
enough be guessed, but not this scent, secret as cancer,
that drifts among the rafters and does not abate, seeps into
hooves, the crooks of legs, coats slick with fear, and waits.

Lascaux

The photographs are separated by the turn

of the page, so to look at one is to conceal

the other. In the first, reindeer flee a panting wolf,

their antlers like unblooming trees upon the cave's wall,

their hooves roots, seeking distant water. In the second,

the scene is repeated, but darkly, stripped of its colors

as if a fire has waned—as if this threadbare encyclopedia

of prehistoric art means to show me what the cave artist

must have seen: figures so nimble by firelight they might be

fleeing some far-off danger, so still in its absence

they nearly vanish. When Ralph Morse entered Lascaux,

the first photographer to do so, he slid into the caves

on a plank of wood cut to the purpose, placed

lengthwise over rock and worn to smoothness by men

whose damp breaths would begin an insuppressible ruin,

covering bison, bulls, and horses with mold. Soon

each herd would be as black as the shadows striping the face

of the Jet Age Man, the Air Force pilot

Morse captured so famously as his skull's contours

were mapped with slatted beams of light. To see

that photo is to recognize an inevitable future, but what,

if I could give it to him, would the Lascaux artist

see there? Tribes from beyond his river, surely,

their faces caked in oils from the fat of cattle,

manganese oxide, soot black. Their spears sharpened.

In another of Morse's photographs, the rotting head

of a Japanese soldier on Guadalcanal, his mouth

open, distended, horrible, rests atop a crippled tank.

A flame held to it illuminates but does not reveal.

Grasses

They are the legs on which
   the world creeps, the tongues

of fallen songbirds, the lances
   of an impossible army, or half-

saluting footmen in liveries
   of moss. Violin strings

in miniature, teased by a vibrato
   of wind, they are the hairs

on Earth's tangled bedsheets,
   a temple torn down each year

and rebuilt. Citizens of a republic
   of beauty, they are a host

of waving hands that will not be
   stilled. On their faces is an unsearchable

history: a great beast is dead, but its
   fingernails are still growing.

Fires and Tents

Secaucus, New Jersey

Snake Hill stands where a glacier once moved blue-veined and trem-
  bling by,
chastened now by graffiti, and wind as unceasing as time's pale hand.
  Up here,
one searches endlessly if at all, turning an eye to the thick rope of
  horizon

stretched lengthwise and vanishing in periphery. One swallows the
  cold air
and is still, or one descends to the checkered valley. When it comes,
  night
is ruthless, settling dust like ground bones on the backs of things,
  collapsing

fires and tents. In the dawn it creeps away sullenly, leaving a
  dampness
wholly wrong for this place before fading west. Each part of this
  morning
suggests some impending . . . some presence. Here, a nye of pheas-
  ants pulls beetles

from the grass, stooping in careful rhythm. A stream reflects the
  building light;
a potter's field undergirds the overpass. Here, the cars circle the
  bodies,
breaking this deep silence and startling the dead into a quickening.

III.

Sestina: Peach Tree

When the peach tree first blossomed, we thought God's hand
had touched us, so beautiful were the buds we saw
bursting from the slender branches: cups of milk marked
with the faintest drops of blood. What did we know of the harvest
to come?—a yield so great mere gusts would bring down
a dozen glowing orbs, so many more than we could hope

to use that our neighbors had to share the bounty. Our hope
in those early weeks was enough peaches to take in hand.
Here was an inheritance, a doctrine to pass down
to our children like teaching one's son to wield a saw,
a legacy as vital as rain. Their only harvest,
to that point, had been televisions, swimming pools. They were
   marked

by it. Never had they dug up stones, cut furrows, marked
the borders of a field. To wrest life from the ground requires hope,
patience, steadfastness, even a kind of love. We wanted that harvest
for them. If we had to, we would take them by the hand.
Better, though, to let them discover for themselves what we saw
every time we looked out the window: that a peach's down

is a sign of ripeness, which means life will move down
and on and upward, sweeping us in its river. Come June, we marked
a change overnight in our garden tree. We saw
its timid band of fruit become a multitude—our hope,
an unlikely seedling, bloom until what hung above us was hand
upon hand of dimpled globes, each a summer harvest

in miniature but together a crop we could never harvest
on our own. Soon enough, the peaches began falling down.
Like oozing sores, they spilt blight, wouldn't heal—dealt a hand
of death across our lawn. Their rotting flesh, which soon marked
our tidy stretch of grass, was putrid as a devil's stool. One can hope
for any number of miracles in this world. But what we saw

from our tree was not abundance but chaos, like a saw
held to a father's throat. A disastrous crop worse than no harvest
at all, it was more than a betrayal. More, even, than a curse. It was
   hope
split open and consumed by flies, or turned to slush and filtered
   down
through the lawn into the soil, a journey that can be marked
but never altered. Our mistake was thinking we could have a hand

in it. If that is what hope does, we will give it no aid, lend no hand
to that which can only make a harvest of us. As for the tree, I marked
the spot. Then I borrowed a neighbor's saw and cut it down.

Lizard

It was only a fence lizard, a brown, mottled thing
that sunned itself upon the walkway, unmoved
by the childish thrust of the broom handle
with which I meant to kill it.
I remember the piercing fear, how quickly curiosity
gave way to revulsion as I imagined—what
did I see there?—its form beneath me, its desperate biology
a puddled stain in which a truth lay
fermenting, dark as mold. Yes,
it meant something to destroy even this body,
so I stilled my hand and called
to my grandmother. Hardly unbending from her gardening,
she crushed it beneath her shoe.

Grammar School: Textbooks

We'd find them stacked large to small
  on the day of our coming: identical bundles
squared upon desks we'd not yet learned
  to outgrow. Into them would go our names,
an appraisal of their condition—a tacit promise
  to do no further harm to these already crippled
wards of the state, shipped yearly
  from home to home, collapsing into dissolution.

The wisest of us had long since discovered
  that ruin is a sliding scale. Judge them *poor*
instead of *fair*, *good* not *very good*, then live exactly
  as you please, taking not a bit of care
at all. Who was checking, really, or would mind
  if one more cover was torn, one more page
defaced? And what was the penalty in that
  economy of childhood? A nickel per mark,
if memory serves—a price well worth the joy,
  so strange and private a pleasure, of destruction.

Grammar School: Evolution

Not even our teachers believed in it, though they tried
    to convince us otherwise, directing with rigid cheerfulness

our attention to illustrations long outdated: solemn menageries
    of beak and bone, man in his elementary stages. All of this

was a test, we knew, to be passed only if we declined
    to look too closely at specimens preserved by the disregard

of our siblings before us. To endure, we had only to close
    our textbooks the moment it was allowed, the swish

of their pages like a serpent in Adam's garden—
    something we might wish to take hold of, but mustn't.

Boxwoods

The boxwoods will not be
made tidy, though I take
my blade to them with every turn
of the season. One long winter,
the shapes I had carved
seemed determined to hold
before bursting into disorder
after a week of rain. Now, even
to approach these thrumming
green hearts is to know
the impertinence of life
and be awed by it. A branch
as strong as bone
has found the socket
between two bricks. It wants
to thrust itself inside my walls,
enter this house in which I
have kept myself for so long
apart. Oh, to touch
the creeping fingers!—
trace the scars whose number
new pruning will soon increase. If there is
falseness in my celebration,
let me be forgiven, allowed a shade
in which to linger, a spirit
renewed in the coolness
of morning, a body
as supple as fine brown roots.

Oil Painting, Artists' Colony

I hardly noticed it at first, the winter landscape
so pale it seemed a portion of the wall, an interruption
only because of the thin lip of its canvas. Frameless,
fixed at awkward height, it skirted easy study,

though its scene, when I looked, was lovely: tidy field
particular with ice, a darker spine of snow cleaving
the earth's surface, rigid vein or road, white chastened
by shadow as rot corrupts an onion's tunic.

And what caught my eyes at last? Only an orchid,
rootless, impossible, clinging to life at meadow's edge,
its face a child's face red with cold, emblem
of nothing save its own inevitable vanishing.

Corner Studio, Artists' Colony

All the best colors are nameless,
the artist tells me, and who am I
to argue? If I propose *sun's lip*,
gold rent by the very depth
of its brilliance, bleeding into orange,
mightn't someone say *buttercup*
or, abstractly, *cheerful*? It's right,
this uncertainty, this casting about
for what to call a representation
of what our eyes tell us we're seeing—
a picture of a picture, revealing
by obscuring. On one canvas,
deep in this dusty studio, a horse
the dappled brown of a finch egg
strides into a foreground damp
with mauve, what I take for
wildflowers. On another, a bee
drowns in its cache of honey, its stinger
grotesquely large, seeming almost
to quiver. Is it *coal*, *jet*, or some other
absence, as far beyond language
as the electric flutter in my limbs—
the thunderstorm outside, within?

Grammar School: Diagramming the Sentence

For an hour, we will admit
  no higher law, learn to guard jealously

its precepts: subordination
  and conjunction, noun and copulae,

slanting lines like
  commandments, or like

the mountain one might descend,
  bearing them.

Minor Prophet

I dreamed this and wrote it down, says the crazy vet
who approaches me on the street, his feet apart
as if braced against God. He is my father's age.
I take the slip of paper from his rusted fingers.
He is urgent. *What's this word?* The forest of his script
has not been pruned. An *x*. An *m* or three broken *t*'s.
A mess of augury. He will not leave. The spirit
is upon him. *What's it say?* His hands are shaking.
What's it say? I cannot tell him. His revelation
is unspeakable. Somewhere he is spreading it still.

The Apostle Paul Extends a Metaphor

Ephesians 2:19–21

The language seems to gather force and leap
Into the air: divine analogy
As spinning top. We, all of us, are those
Whom God has "fitly framed together" as
His holy temple. Still, Paul wonders if
The metaphor is incomplete, as though
A Roman mile had lost its thousandth pace.
Might masonry alone suggest a torpor
Or stillness unbecoming of the bride
Of Christ? Are we not rather restive deer,
Great leopards in a pack, or mourning doves
Lamenting these long lives? The great man knows
His craft will be declined. Best close the scroll.
There will be time for art another day.

Wax Bullet

*None of the firing squad will ever know for sure if he fired a
lethal shot.* —BBC News

For executioners you cover guilt,
Concealing it with what the bee has spilt.
You are the bride the wretched take to bed,
The hungry child who feasts upon their dread.
You are the cliff from which the hopeful leap,
The rocking hand that lulls them to their sleep,
The patient mother whispering a grace,
The god who stoops to show a holy face.
Within your clotted chambers lies a jewel,
A cleansing logic like a cleansing pool.
You will not penetrate a mortal heart,
Nor tear a gunman's righteousness apart.
You are a father, son, and holy ghost.
The man who doesn't need you needs you most.

Conjunctivitis

Let it be plucked out,
this orb whose scales
might finish a witch's
broth, whose film is
an aphid's sticky sap.
Split its thin tissue;
untie its binding
ribbons; snuff the worm
in its wriggling dirt.
Place it on the tongue—
see how it swells
the throat! Clip its
meridian of fire;
sew it into the pocket
of a drowning man.
Release its colony
of serpents, their flesh
the beams of a blood
moon. Rinse it
in brine, crush it,
or swallow it
entire, this eye
of leviathan
so heavy,
piercing,
pungent,
pink.

Offering

When Jehovah drew near Moses to kill him,
Zipporah cut loose the foreskin of their son

with a flint knife, threw the flesh, meager
as a wisp of straw, at Moses's feet. This morning,

not to circumvent God's wrath but in concession
to an ancient habit, we place our son beneath

the doctor's steady hands, her instruments' expert
gleaming—receive him back so nearly whole,

surrenderer of nothing, bestower of no offering
because he cannot understand to miss it.

Miniature Book Collection, Sweet Briar College

Among them are volumes utterly bereft
   of irony: a Lutheran hymnal; a collected

Shakespeare, dollhouse thin. Perhaps
   they were assembled for a child's room,

doled out to daughters solitary, formal,
   or plucked at once—fleeting impulse—

from an antiquer's booth, the proprietor
   barely willing to let them go.

However they congregated, they sit now
   forgotten, lost behind glass, protective

of the oils that will destroy them:
   last vestiges of a dozen generations of fingers.

Proverb

The wolf who tries the lake and drowns,
   the ewe slain in its April down,

will, resurrected, lie together,
   and gambol in a greater heather.

The knife will hold no keenness then,
   the savage arrow find no wren,

nor maids submit to passing lust,
   nor captives anymore be trussed.

The brackish pool will there be sweet,
   the sanctifying hymn complete,

all song and poetry made well
   in that desireless citadel.

No longer will this fire burn.
   There will be no more Baals to spurn.

There will be nothing yet undone
   beneath that ceaseless midnight sun.

The wolf will taste no more of blood,
   nor soldiers suffocate in mud,

nor any man refuse this landing:
   this peace that passeth understanding.

Art Student

It was not quite surprise, not only wonder
   with which I watched him give meaning

to the clay, or lend it. A regular model,
   I had already learned that little he did

could be counted as permanent. The figures
   quickened from the dead element could live

only briefly, and then only as parts: sure torso,
   certain arm, hand too perfect to destroy,

destroyed anyway. This was merely practice.
   The trick was to hone something like memory

in the fingers, tune them to movements
   so familiar he could carry a conversation

as he worked, laugh even as he folded the forms
   in on themselves and began again. What do I know

of such business? That even now it is difficult
   to concede the unmaking, the way each member

broke beneath gestures so nearly careless, all
   that my body meant, until it didn't.

Watching Daybreak on the Savannah

One hundred miles south and to the east,
Oglethorpe and Tomochichi bartered for use
of the river. Here the earth is host
to more recent dead, bones
bound by a whisper of tissue
but bound still, deposited and left for
the rending of their parts to ashes.
The ground hasn't recovered
from the intrusion. It buckles and swells,
its grass untended since the dissolution
of the church that crumbled years ago, kept
the stones and the memories of the dead. Now,
weeds touch the names themselves and may cover
this place one day if left to. I come here
to acknowledge something—to pay
a passing tribute to whatever lives
alongside the longleaf pines, the spiral ladies-tress
sprung from a grave, feeding. The sunrise odor
chokes this morning: wet hair, bleach cut
to the smallest factor. Mosquitos breed
amidst the vagueness of the holy. Below, the fog
should hold like a transparent skin
to the river but instead drifts away.
The water is raw beneath it.

Sunday Sermon

So here again we come with all our sins
Broad blown, stinking to heaven. We concede
The good in one another fitfully,
Neglect what we have promised, turn away
When turning inward might occasion pain.
Like beasts of burden that each year must pull
A little harder to advance their load,
We put our backs into the work. We call
This love and are not wrong to do so. When
The pastor climbs into the pulpit, I
Give you my hand, this palm and grip that you
Have known so well, that used to fairly throb
With certainty and youth. Your other hand
Now grasps the bulletin, that blank expanse
Where sermon notes are tucked into the soil
Of each believer's comprehension, such
As it is. Hebrews 4:15 will be
Our text today: Christ tempted so completely
That he is able to commiserate
With all his lowly flock. We know the verse,
Accept the truth of it, yet even minds
That God is sanctifying can be prone
To wander, as the hymnist says. An hour
Or two will see us safely home, reduced
From holiness to all the cognizance
Of age: that bodies shrink and sag and turn
Against themselves; that muscles atrophy;
That we could live another forty years
Inside these prisons, bound to one another
By habit, love, commitment, and a fear
That neither of us cares to name. Your notes
Have nearly filled the page by now, and I

Can't help but glance at your neat letters, like
A line of clerics leaning to one side.
Christ stooped into the muck with his creation.
Temptation came his way, but did he taste
What we discover daily? If I could
Contribute to your jottings I might add
A line or two. He knew our sorrows. But
He never married. He never grew old.

Patriotic Concert, Covenant Presbyterian Church

To whom could we sing such songs
if not to soldiers? And who else
to thank for this silence
before the swoop of the conductor's
baton, bargain struck
at ten thousand Leipzigs and Normandies,
brought home in wretched haversacks
or the tin-lined insides
of canteens? What was bought
in bleeding fields inhabits the gothic
sprawl of this cathedral,
where multitudes in colored glass
lean away from Christ's
sermon to hear the chiff
of the organ, the whale swallowing Jonah
tilts its curious head. In a dozen
drab rehearsals, our vowels
had to be stretched, leaned
upon, lest our words go soft. Now,
even earthbound octaves
seem to scrape the ceiling's tongue-
and-groove, find gaps
through which to seep into
the night's held breath. In the front pew,
a man in uniform is plainly
weeping. His wife holds his sleeve
as if he, too, might vanish. Into what
percussive dream is he
falling, what grievous canticle, and how
honor him but reach the highest
notes purely? And go out.
And bear children.

Acknowledgments

I am grateful to the editors of the following journals, in which some of these poems previously appeared: *32 Poems, Atlanta Review, Barrow Street, The Believer, Birmingham Poetry Review, Blackbird, Chattahoochee Review, Controlled Burn, Copper Nickel, Ekstasis, Epoch, Greensboro Review, Hiram Poetry Review, Image, The Journal, Mid-American Review, National Review, The New Criterion, Nimrod, Notre Dame Review, Poems for Ephesians, Puerto del Sol, Regarding Arts and Letters, Sewanee Review, Southern Humanities Review, Sou'wester, Summerset Review, Tar River Poetry*, and *Two Review*.

"Lizard," which first appeared in *Tar River Poetry*, was reprinted in *The Southern Poetry Anthology: Tennessee* (2013). "Miniature Book Collection, Sweet Briar College" (*Sewanee Review*) was featured on *Poetry Daily*. "Minor Prophet" (*Hiram Poetry Review*) was reprinted in *American Society: What Poets See* (2012). "The Timpanist" (*32 Poems*) was reprinted in *How to Write a Poem* (2015). "Watching Daybreak on the Savannah" (*Puerto del Sol*) was reprinted in *Stone, River, Sky: An Anthology of Georgia Poems* (2015).

In addition, thanks are due to Trevecca Nazarene University, the Tennessee Arts Commission, the Virginia Center for the Creative Arts, the Sewanee Writers' Conference, and Anders Carlson-Wee for myriad kindnesses during the composition and revision of this manuscript. Thanks to D.S. Martin for choosing this book for the *Poiema Poetry Series*. Finally, thank you to Bobby C. Rogers, without whose example and friendship this book would not exist.

The Poiema Poetry Series

The Book of Bearings by Diane Glancy
In a Strange Land anthology edited by D.S. Martin
What I Have I Offer With Two Hands by Jacob Stratman
Slender Warble by Susan Cowger
Madonna, Complex by Jen Stewart Fueston
No Reason by Jack Stewart
Abundance by Andrew Lansdown
Angelicus by D.S. Martin
Trespassing on the Mount of Olives by Brad Davis
The Angel of Absolute Zero by Marjorie Stelmach